9.95

The Birds of Pompeii

The Birds of Pompeii

POEMS BY John Ciardi

THE UNIVERSITY OF ARKANSAS PRESS
Fayetteville

0 5 0 8 5 6 4 2

Acknowledgment is made to the following magazines that first published
some of these poems:
Poetry, *The Pearl* (Denmark), *The Little Balkans Review*, *Journal of The Dante
Society of Massachusetts*, *New Letters*, *Northern Lights*, and *Far Hills Review*.

LIBRARY OF CONGRESS CATALOGING IN PUBLICATION DATA

Ciardi, John, 1916–
   The Birds of Pompeii.
   I. Title.
PS3505.I27B5 1985   811'.52   84-28077
ISBN 0-938626-44-2
ISBN 0-938626-45-0 (pbk.)

For John Roger and Dorothy Fredland;
    she for tolerating him,
    he for tolerating me,
    in old friendship that grows better.

Contents

Happiness

Happiness

Whenever I waken and this animal,
in glandular reprieve, curls to the sun
as glad as trout are wet, as slugs crawl,
as fledglings nest in stink, each in its own
lack of confusion outright to a success
that does what it does because it does it because

it knows no other and what works is joy
in the habit of the fitted habitat—
then I am no man but indigenous boy
bright running fields across, until the fat
and failing man after the boy stirs wheezy,
his body a separate mind, his mind uneasy.

What am I doing dabbling here in bliss
as if with a child whore who pouts for more
when I am dead? I am too old for this.
Yet, like an Easter in a candy store,
wafts of spiced angels shimmer and invite
all greed to gorge, and give it appetite.

Inanely happy, humanly out of place,
I sip black coffee and the morning news,
the collected daily rages of the race,
till everything is as bad as it always was.
And I grow serene. I have not lost my mind.
I recognize our disastrous humankind

and am in control of my own wits again
to live and die in accurately. Amen.

The Glory

> If it does not return, as seems likely now,
> and Heaven is a broken appointment, yet
> I have attended it with all I know
> of protocol. And attend. And will not forget.

My wife said, "There's an angel at the door!"
Something certainly had taken the air.
A suffusion like mountain mist with sun at its core,
its arrows drawn and blazing. So the rare

subsumes the usual. She herself had never
appeared more radiant. Our best glasses
burst in high C haloes. May I ever
be open to seizure. As a life amasses

the power of its choices. As no part of Heaven
can be intrusive. Yet I had nothing on
but a frayed robe, hadn't shaved, hadn't even
finger-combed my hair. What could I have done

to receive magnificence? With so many means
to annunciation why would the messenger come
in a sunburst before breakfast? before a man's
dentures had warmed? "Please say I am not at home,"

I begged, "If he/she/it—whatever they
turn out to be in essence—is free at ten,
I shall make it an homage to rearrange my day
to the convenience of Heaven."

                              Since then
I have shaved, showered, dressed, and waited till the sky
clotted the trees. I have sat here needled numb
by congested hope, my shoes shined holy, my tie
precise as a Credo. Let the Glory come

if I am fit to receive it in the dress
and form that is its due. My wife and son
wait with me in their observant best. Unless
the Glory is met in ritual, there is none.

Praise

If the art is praise, do saints have it common
with the lion gutting a zebra and then sunning?
A purr like a river of soft gravel comes on.
Cubs are safe from wrath with that river running.
He will even twitch his tail and let them pounce
on the dancing pompom. There were such gods once.

Or something like a general benevolence
extending even to zebras in some way
that hones the herd and that mutes violence
to a sort of sexual shudder—as saints pray
in a terror without which they wouldn't know how to be.
The art is, finally, sensuality.

With the difference that saints and those who admire them
make the good rape of time a masturbation.
If it has to be self-induced, it grows tiresome.
Nature always suffers in translation.
Always, in the original, the art
is every creature's response to the habitat

in which it is most possible. But the saint
is never home. He does not live his praise.
He sends it to some Gothic *poste restante*,
himself mailed there in time to no address.
Praise is the art-in-common of not dying.
And note that no saint ever ate a lion.

Posthumous

The Honor Guard at the Tomb of the Unknown Citizen
went AWOL to chase naked Virtue screaming
to classified rape in the darks of the Pentagon.

An ambivalence of cops guards and suspects me
till I buy my tickets to the Policemen's Ball
and am given my Bumper Sticker. I affirm.

But can we choose what we know of one another?
I am not in Rahway because I am White. The Blacks
are there for having defaced the Bumper Stickers

that protect my chrome, my shining innocence.
But I do not walk Newark at night, and I keep a gun
and a German Shepherd for what night-walks me.

I declare a straddled statistic. Enjambed to it,
I vote my choice of no choice. I confess
it is I, love maddened, who have been rescuing Virtue

from the Honor Guards of our menacing monuments
to rape her myself. We were engaged once.
If she lives, I mean to marry her—I swear it.

But I am a known liar. And she by now
is pregnant with the rapist's child. Can this
be the marriage made in Heaven?

                              Yet let me only
not be most threatened by what I most must have.
I cannot bear to be guarded in this tomb,
and do not dare be left in it alone.

Sometimes the Bumper Stickers become a dream
and I almost waken from it, almost ready
to love unscared. But why be ridiculous?

True or False

Real emeralds are worth more than synthetics
but the only way to tell one from the other
is to heat them to a stated temperature,
then tap. When it's done properly
the real one shatters.

                        I have no emeralds.
I was told this about them by a woman
who said someone had told her. True or false,
I have held my own palmful of bright breakage
from a truth too late. I know the principle.

Memoir of a One-Armed Harp Teacher

Of my three certainly most impassioned students,
one lived over a disco and could not practice,
one split her calluses red and was admonished
by dermatologists, one married a psychic
and took to listening. There are always available
good, or good enough, reasons for putting by
the incompatible, the painful, the unserviceable.
One decides what is important by what one does.

But the most demanding instrument forgives least.
I, who have been the teacher of many failures,
do not blame everything on the student body.
I could have done better with both hands. Perhaps
with an unamputated mind and the heart for it.
Passion is a crippling hobby, a killing trade.

Quirks

I. *Breakfast on the Patio*

Not much but something. Before the morning glories
closed on the patio and my coffee went cold
whole wafts of monarchs blew from histories
that happened only to be told and retold
by marshmallow bushes in the gingerbread glade
where Snow White sleeps, half holy and half mad.

Well, one or two at a time, but over and over
surfed the last white edges as they shrank.
Fluffs so slight they do not fly but hover.
Yet I had read—in the *Geographic*, I think—
they breed mostly in Mexico, and some
in Monterey. How far so little can come!

Someone statistical has found a way
to mark them weightlessly, and has traced their skim
as far as Nova Scotia. But one that day
paid off the wind. It fell into my cream
and twitched off the last dust of its last tatter.
I forked it out to sun on my bread platter,

but it had frayed forever, having left
a whorl from some lost fingerprint in the bowl.
I spooned it for Hansel and Gretel and drank a draught
from their first Sabbath. Tasteless. But all in all
a kiss to change a frog. Then the last flower shut.
The phone rang. And the day trekked on and out.

II. *That Afternoon I Remembered*

There is a photo of Walt Whitman posed
with a butterfly aflutter on one finger.
The Bard as the Olympian *quelque chose*

of his own fairy tale. I, the humdinger
who breakfasted on butterfly dust with Zeus,
or Jack and Jill, cite Walt as my excuse

for letting my impulse flicker grandiose.
In meager fact, Charles Feinberg bought a trunk
that had been Whitman's, and among old clothes,
the boots Puss wore, and miscellaneous junk,
found folded flat the paper butterfly
from the finger Walt had poked into God's eye.

That's more than I had pretended. I was still
halfway into and halfway out of sleep
when I spooned up the last dust of what fell
ex machina—a notion that wouldn't keep
to be collected, a least creature touch
back through drowsy nowhere to nothing much.

Two Dry Poems

Drought

Will prayer temper the wind to the shorn lamb?
Lambs are not for shearing. Nor the wind sent.
The ewe grieves. Or it sounds like grief. The ram
hugs a small dune to windward, its cusp rent
by the jut of one stiff leg. The ripple lifts
a feather from the fleece. The dust drifts
over the dead creature where it fell.
My tongue cracks when I call thee, Israel.

Praying for Rain in a Cracked Field

Few get wet by it. Nevertheless, the fact
of declaring hope in the best words one can find
has been known to help congregations adjust to the act

of remaining dry. Nothing speaks to the wind.
The words are spoken from and for and to
the congregation. As hope is dew to the mind.

As religion is above all something to do
when there is nothing to be done. As a poem
is also a something-nothing going through

the motions of saying itself to rest, to some
knowledge of what species dreams a kingdom
and, while the words lift, has its kingdom come.

Interstellar

FM Wireless Intercom. REALISTIC.
U.S. Tested. PLUG 'N TALK.

I

I have an intercom in my attic study
for my wife to beep and say in domestic static,
"Dinner's ready." Decoded, that means, "Ten minutes
to find a stopping place and to wash your hands."

Last night at two a baby's primary wail
came from it, then some secondary parents
mouthing and mouthing, voices without words.
Had I tuned in Bethlehem without its beasts?

The baby cries in Norwegian. Not *wah! wah!*
but In-GA! In-GA! My daughter, while still a bundle,
was a Norwegian. But this was no fantasy.
I called my amplified son in and said, "Listen!"

"I don' know wha' youah pickin' up," he said,
"but that's for sure a baby, with whatch'd call
youah standud parents doin' a heavy nothin'!"
Changeling! Must hope end in genetic malfunction?

Then, hope reborn, there's a monitor by a crib
and I'm tuned in.—But none of my neighbors have
        babies.
Boys and girls but no babies. I asked the mailman.
"Young couples can't afford this block," he said.

He made me hate my address. We bought in time
and couldn't afford to now. Working till dawn,
I find myself waiting for that defined baby
and its vague parents. Then, when I have forgotten,

they crackle in from the Horseheads, and I'm as happy
as if love were a contractual reality
and hope an escrow. I'm what a voyeur would be
at a radio-telescope. In-GA! In-GA!

Had I faith enough, I could build a church around it
and its prattling parents. I did once but still mumble
for lacking of the solving words. A *paternoster*
reduced to *patter*.* And still that primary wail.

I am moved to thank someone for I don't know what.

II

4:30 A.M. the next night. My ghost baby
wails me up from a book that has less to say
than In-GA! In-GA! At five it is screaming bubbles
out of its throat. Magma. Its clod parents
have not yet stirred. Have they tuned out attendance?
If I can hear, they could. I dial full volume,
press the talk button and thunder, "This is God.
My baby is crying and where are you?"—No answer.
The baby whimpers out. The rest is silence.

Dare I suppose the thunder sounded through?
that someone just outside this neighborhood
has had a religious experience? With luck,
and our species' specific taste for exaggeration,
how long would it take for my voice to become a rumor;
the rumor, a Bible; and the Bible, Law?
I have a cousin who could run that course
in any twenty pre-beatified seconds.

This is the parable of the leaden parents
of the golden child. And of how God's reveille

---

*As all should know, though too many do not, *patter* derives from the
priestly mumbling of *paternoster*, as if "patter noster."

might gild us all. The connection, however, is tricky.
Even at full volume there is no answer.
But the baby has stopped wailing. Power is power.
I do not even press the button. I whisper,
"Child, you have been heard where sleep begins."

III

Three nights now and nothing wails "Me! Me!"
"Dinner's ready!" the box squawks. Message enough
to feast the South Sahara. I press the key
and lean to the box to answer, "Coming, Love."
It turns to static. But something crackles through
the interferences jamming all we do

since God changed frequencies or went off the air.
I wait with no insistence and start to forget.
Then, on the fourth night, there is something there.
A squeak in the Zodiac just before first light
when dreams are truest. Then, echoing from a star,
the word that began the world: *In-GA! In-GA!*

God and its parents are a space static
behind the star-child's nova. I eavesdrop
under a gas-roofed galaxy. My attic
glows with light years. Then a switch goes *clop!*
and we're back at our two ends of a broken ray
that almost promised there might be something to say.

Poetry

Death is everywhere in it. Yet
it may be the most act of not-
dying. Listen when there is time.
Make time till it is still enough
to hear across water and time
the tilting band of the *Titanic*.
Nearer my Oom to Pah! The tuba
pumping behind prayer over
and over. The North Atlantic
already in their shoes. But one more
time long as there is time over
and over, the music holding
to itself, holding everything
not long, but for its while,
forever. The cornets throwing
their lifeline high and clear
over the cold bald misted curve
nowhere, the tuba pumping
the prayer behind the prayer,
an echo off the ice.
                    Oompah!

An Interruption

Aphrodite phoned. Could I come over?
I was, at that moment, writing a poem about her
and how I "yearned"—that was the word—to be with her.
Could I interrupt the writing? I begged off.

She hung up in a huff. I cannot believe
she will be calling soon again. So be it.
There comes a season for saying only what's possible.
I ask nothing but to say it right, if I can.

It is when nothing comes to mind that "yearning"
gets sucked into the vacuum. I knew
all the void next day of bone revision
it is a vacuum, and that nothing fills it.

It is madness to say no to her for a word's sake.
Madness to scrub for the word and not find it.
She, too, is mad, but if I do not sit
and "yearn" to say her—always that word again—

she may find she is not there when she thinks to call.
She probably will not think to. I will wait.
She will learn in her own vacuum, if I tire,
how Goddesses, above all, must be said.

Going to the Dogs

The head of the German Shepherd I have now
is bigger than all the pup I started with.

He looks dangerous, and used to be. A wolf
and territorial. All the lock we needed.

It hurts to see him age and gentle creaky.
He follows from room to room to grunt, and sprawl

three feet away. Dependency needn't touch.
Even the puppy used to fight off my lap.

It wanted its own four feet on its own ground.
So we came to an understanding I have respected:

We are on one another's side but never
one another. Let be and let be.

He does grovel for food. I can remember
what cockroach jobs I stank through once for bread,

saying yessir to the mongrel bloats that paid me.
I know dependency, not to like it. It's his

—it's anyone's—universe as much as mine
by an equal ranking so long disarranged

it won't dress right again. It's my turn now
to pay, and I pay, and he takes. That's in our contract.

It will be over soon. I'll probably live
to bury him, but not whole campaigns longer.

I have grown to need him sprawled there on the floor
of every room I come to. The sound of his breathing

keeps keeping time for me. When I think I need
his love, or obedience, or whatever response

I think I need, I am happy to be shameless.
I reach for the dog biscuits I keep cached

all over the house, and he is utterly mine.
Movies and most of the women's magazines

my wife subscribes to, argue for more. But why?
We want one another for what each needs from each.

What's wrong with bribery? I'm a democrat:
I want no special privilege for myself

that can't be had, at need, by anyone else
for the same bribe, *pro rata*. I need. He needs.

Amo, amas, amat.—I have never tried
nibbling dog biscuit. It could come to that.

Right now it would be too much like eating money,
and that I have to save for my last whore

or be left to the unanswerable unanswered,
even by a gut that pretends love.

Barmecide Feast

I have been told, and have been glad to hear,
of the resonance and radiance of God's intention
arching the canopy over wakening man,
bending the branches with fruiting, frothing
first waters with pearl fishes, gilding the wheat spikes
of the bee-hymned land, uncoiling
the goose from the font of the egg, the spline
of the onion from its sheath, and welling
mint springs from deep earth, all
in a single happening more than occurrence, done
round to its doing as a wheel
spins wheels that spin wheels till all plenty
is motion from one center.

                  I spoke of this
to priests and rabbis who had understood
the feast of intention, who could quote
more calories than I could eat, and touch
the water of the wedding to wine,
the germ of birth to the risen bread of angels.

They sat me in the vortex of His bounty.
Their servants brought gold dishes beaten weightless
and steaming like censers with miraculous nothing.
They brought me goblets carved from a single topaz
brimming with radiant vapors. Seven poets

blinded by God served me described fish.
And while their lutes shook out the bleeding seeds
of conceived pomegranates, I starved supposing
my animal could range on feasted assumptions.

Diary Entry

I was in a mood for disaster
but couldn't afford much.
At the God store I counted out
my last three worn *perversos*
and ordered an ounce of avalanche.
His thumb on the scale,
it came to one grain of sand
which He blew in my eye,
perhaps to teach me something.

Which He did. A rule of thumb:
all else being equal,
I'll not be caught, not soon again,
trying to do business on His scale.

Elegy for a Sweet Sharpy

When everyone else dropped in a handful of dirt,
I dropped a Preciso pocket calculator
with Sure-Seal Everlast Batteries. Chances are
not even you will figure a way out,
but how could I not give you a chance to try?

It can't be any harder than smelling the lilies.
And I still half expect—enough to dream it—
the ground will open a crack and you'll sneak through
spinning the angles of one more everyone-wins
razzle-dazzle. Give it your sneakiest shot!

Who would not welcome proof the spirit lives?
I've put down thirty-nine ninety-nine plus tax
you'll come up Easter yet. On anyone else
that goes as a sucker bet. But win or lose,
it is longer than lilies to be remembered in kind.

Domestic Sonnet

The cat gave birth to an adder. The dog died
of roughing up the unknown. The mynah bird
denaturalized him in three undeleted
expletives. The mice, if any heard,
stayed in the walls of instinct. Something
must speak for nature when everything else here
bends off its genes.—The last Easter duckling,
for instance (the other five died), that drinks beer
and quacks for pretzel bits while Father Dust Pan
follows it brushing up the dotted lines
across everything. (Splatterfamilial man
in his turd-stippled castle of dotty scions,
as much changelings as brood.) But what the hell,
it works somehow, never entirely well.

Socializing with a Creature

"Creature," I said to the blue jay nesting
in the ilex bush at my window,
"why so visibly? You are more than welcome,
but do you suppose our midnight skunk,
our garbage can raccoon, and our ghost possum
are blind, earless, noseless, and hate eggs?"

She sat to her doing. I was under glass
in another continuum. When her cock came,
a twitching snarl in his beak, I still
did not exist. She flicked and the tangle
straightened down a surviving reflex.
And he left and came. And she sat.

I think I have seen two eggs. I have not trimmed.
The nest has blurred into new growth, not enough.
Do they really know what they are doing?
They could at least have started
a foot down into the thick of it,
or higher, in some crotch of better instinct.

"Creature," I said to unnatural foolishness,
"some forty or fifty thousand years ago—
whatever years are—my egg-sucking parents
gave up instinct to take a chance on reason
and lost their balance forever. You, I had thought,
are still spun on the original gyroscope.

"Or are you, too, tip-tilted? Is the tilt
something we knocked? Have you, creature,
taken example from us? I can believe
in an idiot presidency. But a stupid nesting?—
Ronald Reagan could have done it better.
I'll lay you grubs to turds you're hatching candy

"for my wife's denatured cat. And be glad to lose.
Or even to hope you'll make it through the night
if I can heap our garbage in your favor.
Do you think there are make-up courses in evolution?
If birds no longer know about being birds,
why not nest on the hardtop and be done?"

Corpus Christi

Once a year in some self-secreting Lent
or Carnival, Gulf lobsters form in chains
and move in ritual. Divers who saw that pageant
went down with cameras and lights. But what explains
the unknown to itself? In a slow, dim,
endless sequence from a Fellini film

I lockstep a last bottom beyond sleep
behind my father moving behind his father.
No way to make a living. But we keep
an appointment with ourselves. If we do not scatter,
sooner or later a shrimper's drag will find
our line of march. It may come from behind,

ahead, or across our linkage, but it comes.
Sometimes it misses. Sometimes it gathers us in
to the feast of something else. A thousand domes
on a thousand roads to a crab-clawed Vatican
are its told buoys. We move under and through
the dark and drift of whatever it is we do.

Leaving Longboat Key

In memory of William Sloane, III

The drawbridge blinks red, yawns. The airport limo
gnashes its teeth and waits. A blown gray scarf
of pelicans flutters high across the water,
then wavers over the edge. A white convertible,
top-down in the glare outside our air-sealed windows
bursts chrome grenades in the heat shimmer. I look,

then look again, having glanced once and by.
—It's true! An instant can be! You are tanned,
a cultivation of tan. What a basking grave
you must have drawn at the lottery! I know
I mustn't speak. That there are rules. But thank you
for what still visits.

                              —The bridge rings and swings shut.
Half-naked fools in a white sloop wave beer cans,
two egrets almost hand in hand above them.
We groan and glide. The light, and everything, changes.
A spangled man in a programmed tan turns right
on a white coral road into the sun.
I touch my inside pocket and feel my ticket.

An Apology for a Lost Classicism

I was writing a *trentesei* for the boat-people
when I ran out of chocolate mints and lost rhyme.
There is no conspiracy against creativity.
One yet notes art must be a precise encounter.
It is possible only at the fullest confluence
within the circumstance of concept and creature.

When I ran out of chocolate mints and lost rhyme
I was alone in grieving for my failure.
The boat-people, adrift in their killing freedom,
cared nothing that the demands of art are total.
They were too busy bailing, and thirst lacks style.
I was alone in grieving for my failure.

There is no conspiracy against creativity.
It is the conceiving creature, not the concept,
falls belittled by its creature-craving.
And also that one's subjects, caught in their agon,
refuse to see that they matter only as instance,
dismissible witnesses to perdurable form.

One yet notes art must be a precise encounter.
I had been nagged from an epic sympathy
by nothing more than the teasing of my sweet tooth.
A stupid insistence. Yet concept must not be riled.
Can be shaped only by undistracted energy
freed of all need to provision its own survival.

It is possible only at the fullest confluence
of analogy and order, whose traditions
testify to us that ideal Greece herself,
our cradle of concept, was raised to the noumenal
on the bones of slaves, whose otherwise pointless *soma*
subtended the *neuros* of the master encounter.

Within the circumstance of concept and creature
I tried to make do with Oreos. But there are
no substitutes for essence. Perhaps tomorrow,
when I buy another paper and infinite mints,
I shall fix these drownings from *incidence* to *summa*,
and need not grieve alone for the boat-people.

At Least with Good Whiskey

She gave me a drink and told me she had tried
to read my book but had had to put it down
because it depressed her. Why, she wanted to know,
couldn't I turn my talent (I raised my glass)
to happier things? Did I suppose it was smart
to be forever dying? Not forever,
I told her, sipping: by actuarial tables
ten years should about do it. See what I mean?
she hurried to say—always that terrible sadness.
Well, maybe, I said. (This is good whiskey, I said.)
But ten years, plus or minus, is not much time
for getting it said—do you see what I mean?—which leaves me
too busy to make a hobby of being sad.

A Damnation of Doves

Where did doves perch before there were telephone wires?
I think they evolved in cemeteries. The dead
might tolerate them. They don't have to hear
that eternal cooing. Yes, Mohammed said
Noah's dove is in Heaven, one of the ten
creature-saints so honored in the Koran

for having done God's will. But tell me how
it managed to break that branch from the olive tree.
What did it use for pruning shears? I know
it was miracle time back there in deep B.C.,
but who would have been offended had a hawk
with a proper cutting beak been assigned the work?

Were there a hawk in Heaven, I'd pray it down
to prune these flocks. That wouldn't interfere
with the balance of nature. And once the work was done
I might manage to rinse this cooing from my ears
by singing hymns, or kneeling to TV,
or whatever does for ritual in A.D.

Finally That
Blue Receding Sphere

Apprehendee Then Exited Vee-hicle

"Sorry," said the cop who had shot me,
"you know how it is with mistaken identity."

I knew. I have never really liked my looks.
I have never really looked as I really am.

Not as I know I'd look if I turned real.
"We all have something to regret," I said.

"Please inform my estate that my last thoughts
were all of her—and, of course, Internal Revenue."

"Hold on," said the sergeant, "there is still the matter
of six expended bullets to be accounted.

You know the regulation shooting form."
"Only four hit," said the cop, "and he's not the man."

"The form is the form. Six fired is six expended.
You will report accordingly. Now to the charges:

He led you to think he was someone else—what's that
but impersonating intent, obstruction of justice

by misleading an officer, and accessory
to damn poor shooting? Read him his rights and book
    him."

"You have the right," said the cop, "to remain silent. . . ."
"Thank you," I told him, "I feel it coming on."

Mutterings

I may have no more to say to my left arm.
We used to be friends till it took to hanging out
with a cervical pinch. Now it sleeps all day
or wakens to needle me. When I try to sleep

it raises foolish questions. I do not care
to be interrogated by my components.
Especially when I am trying to sleep.
I don't mind honest questions—what have I to hide?

(Forgive me: strike that question. It took this race
billions of lives to code me devious.
I will not dishonor my making by pretending
not to know father and mother. I meant to say:)

What can I have to hide from my left arm?
Except what my right is doing? And it is blameless.
It is helping me write this poem. For better or worse,
a poem is exactly where the devious ends.

(Forgive me again: by the split tongues of my people,
there is no point past lying. All saying's bent
to its own forked words, our own, not of our making.
. . . And yet to lie some halfway to a truth! . . .)

But on with it. When my sacro-iliac
blathered me off my legs a neurosurgeon
harangued them back to me. There can at times
be a winning argument, if only a jargon.

Another logician hanged me from a door
in a slip-on gibbet: a noose from chin to crown,
a counterweight dangling like a corpse from a pulley.
He called it traction. I sat and discussed it with Plato,

stretching myself to noumena till I retched.
I am tired of the mutterings of my own sub-surfs.
I howled them down, a pink pill under my tongue.
But my speech perfected, I had nothing to say.

And what now? Sometimes I look down at my knuckles.
Are they thinking to pop a question? I'm bone-weary
of being nagged to death from inside. And still
the questions come, and one of them is the answer.

Thursday Also Happens

Yesterday when the leaves blew off the elm
I looked out the window of the third-floor landing
eye to eye with the squirrel that used to be there—
and saw a silk hat on the upper trunk.

"There's a top hat in the elm," I told my wife.
"Why?" she said, "This isn't Thursday, is it?"
"As a matter of fact, it is," I told her. "Drat!"
she said, "I've known all day I was late for something!"

"Take the car," I said. It wasn't Thursday.
I wanted her out of the way while I climbed the ladder,
as I knew I must. She would have screamed, "You'll fall!"
And I would have fallen. I am subject to suggestion.

But once she was gone, I could make it. I said to myself,
"Of course you can make it." And having said so, I did.
I had guessed the topper was hung on a twig. It wasn't:
it was fixed to the trunk by a shingle-nail through the brim.

I had no hammer and had to rip it off
leaving a silken inkstain on the bark
with a nailhead in it. The hat was buff-new.
The leather band was stamped in gold, "A. T."

Arturo Toscanini? The silk of the crown
bore an embroidered label: "Strega—Milano."
It confirmed my guess. When I reached in, a dove
unfurled in my hand. Thank God it wasn't a rabbit:

I couldn't have carried it down and the fall would have
        made
a military splash in my pachysandra.
I didn't reach in again. I let the dove go.
The thing kept flying back with olive branches.

"Stop it!" I said, "It wasn't that wet a summer.
I don't much like green olives. Why make a Bible
of what began as simple curiosity?"
There was also the fact that heights make me dizzy:

I had to get down. And since I needed both hands
for my death grip on the ladder, I put the hat on.
I should have known better. My wife came into my head.
I saw in greater detail than was necessary

what she had been late for. So Arvin Tremblow!
—Imagine thinking it might have been Toscanini!—
"I'd best get down," I said. And found myself down.
I knew then. "This is bigger than we are," the dove said.

When I went indoors after pointing the cat at the dove,
the phone was ringing. "It's bigger than we are," it said.
"I know," I told her. "Will you need the car?"
—"Only to fetch my things."—"I'll have them ready."

"Thank you for understanding," she said. I shrugged.
"It happens," I said. "The leaves blow off and one sees.
Drive carefully. This rush hour traffic kills."
Later I thanked the sergeant who phoned to tell me.

Then I phoned Fay Morticians and made the
     arrangements.
Then I sat down with a fresh bottle of bourbon
and thought of Natalie Krink. I said aloud,
"Am I only thinking through my hat?"—"Not really,"

she said, coming in like spring, "but take it off."
So I took it off and it was my wife again.
"You finished the whole bottle!" she said. I nodded.
A man must do what he can when his love leaves him.

Ward Three: Faith

I had only a tack hammer, an ice pick, faith,
and His command to me in an unknown tongue.

The Creation began with less. I wrapped sandwiches,
filled a Coke bottle with water, went into the desert.

Five days later at Cathedral Canyon
I ate my last dried liverwurst and waited

in the five o'clock furnace. The News would be on the air
from another Time Zone, a propitious hour

for all vibrations. Hell's own heat squeezed me,
but He sent the shadow of the western cliff.

I turned to praise Him, striking rock with my bottle,
and water flowed from it. The desert did not bloom

but a last ray blazed a point on the eastern rim
where all else was the twilight of desolation,

and the voice one hears at will when he wills it enough
said, "Raise ye here an altar unto Me."

"With an ice pick, a tack hammer, and no water!"
I editorialized from Original Sin.

A shadow passed over my soul. "Delete!" I cried.
"Make read: by faith alone shall ye move mountains!"

*　*　*

The Jeep found me under a wheel of buzzards.
So I was told. I remember some presence descending.

But the telling was fractured. Words and no
    understanding.
A survey plane from the National Park Service

had noted a spire of marble burning white
on Black Rock Mesa, circled close with glasses,

and seen what appeared to be enormous inscriptions
in an unknown language. The University

had, at a guess, sent out an Aztec specialist.
He had taken photos and rock chips, measured and
      mapped.

He understood nothing. But Schlitz flowed from him
and Kraft's Provolone and Wonder Bread. The Lord

prepared a table before me with Gulden's Mustard
but gave no comfort to the unbeliever.

"God knows what it is," said the Aztec. Even then—
the truth on his lips—he could not hear and know it.

"Have ye asked of the godly?" I telepathized
when I had bloomed again. He answered aloud:

"At a State University?"—It was so at Babel.
"Is there no seer among you?" I beamed again.

"Not within my discipline," said the Aztec.
"We'll know what it is when we get it on instruments."

"O ye of little faith," I beamed a last time,
"how then have ye heard voices when none has spoken?"

"When none has . . . !" said the Aztec, and stopped
      refuted.
Then spoke into his radio and it spoke

revealing itself in the tongues of the air, saying,
"John, John, thy labors are over. Come rest in Me."

And I came from the desert having heard my name,
and was met, and was led to this rest, and am feasted.

They bring me Spam and I eat, and that is His body; and Kool-Aid and I drink, and that is His blood.

At night the tube goes black, but I find the clicker here in my hand, and I need only choose.

Middle Class Poem

Some of the time when nothing ever happens
but the phone again to prove you're a wrong number
(or why would you answer, having nothing to say?)

you open the junk mail and your computerized name
solicits you three misspelled times a page
with promises of a hope God could not green

and hasn't bothered to make to the Haitian babies
whose mortality rate is not available
for direct sales mail promotion—or who would want it?

So you tape their mouths, stuff them in body bags,
and pile them on the curb. But the truth leaks out.
A uniformed saint breaks in and delivers a summons

for littering God's intention. There are signs
that someone is doing so. It could be you.
You can see for yourself your door is off its hinges.

Why argue? You could tell yourself, and believe it,
you have made some effort to be orderly.
But was it ever enough? When you answer the summons,

what have you to expect from municipal court
but local expedience? And the question remains:
which is the intention and which the litter?

You could appeal, but the law is itself confused,
and saints on their patrols are not debaters.
They are quick to interpret questions as resistance.

It is best to avoid law as best one can.
Haitians die every day of being too many
to prove their right. Or they become wrong

when the court of intention will not hear their appeal
on the grounds that death, by voiding interest,
cancels grievance. Better pay up and live.

You phone your inside man at the signatory
end of the Constitution. He refers you
to the party secretary at City Hall

who pleads a previous commitment to civic duty
but can accept campaign funds, and will *pro rata*
do what he can for the justification of justice.

He does manage to get the charge dismissed.
Sometimes it works. But the littering does not stop.
And tomorrow the door-smashing saints are back.

But you're not there. Your procedures have been
        foreclosed.
You couldn't afford both freedom and your mortgage.
You tell yourself you know which must come first,

but you have been wrong before with no surprise.
Not quite as wrong as you'd expect to have been
had you been born in Haiti, but wrong enough.

Friends

A man from a house not far who rode the train
I used to take to New York till I stopped going,
though we still nodded, and later I learned his name
when my wife met his, and once when we were throwing
an even-up munch-and-swozzle open house
they came, and a month later invited us

to his country club, so later we asked them to mine
and were next-to-last one year in the member-guest,
and became, as you might say, friends, or from time to time
had drinks, or when we were out with someone else,
and they were, we bought their table drinks around,
and they waved and came over, and once, having eaten,
    we found

he had picked up our check, so we sent champagne,
a magnum, and stopped for a glass with them because
we were doing well, or at least feeling no pain,
which led us to think we were friends, and there certainly
    was
no reason not to, and none whatever to know
more about him except as a good Joe,

—died, omitting flowers for the cancer fund,
so we sent a donation card and went to the viewing,
and Tuesday morning to Woodlawn, and stood around,
and a decent later we phoned her to say we were doing
nothing much and how about dinner, but she
had been disconnected, had moved to Marathon Key

we were told by the agent who had sold the house
and sent her the check. So on our way to Key West
my wife tried to phone, but couldn't, and had to guess
she had maybe remarried, so we drove the rest
of the way to our condo and said a big hello
to all the people there we think we know.

Going Late to New Brunswick

When you have exactly two dollars and the fare
is two forty-five, it always starts to rain.

You make it to Penn Station, the leatherbound
edition of *Consolations* under your coat.

So philosophy is safe, and could even save you
the wet walk from Metuchen to New Brunswick.

But have you ever tried selling Boethius
at midnight in Penn Station? With cops watching?

As a philosopher, you have noted from nature
that all tickets are collected at Newark.

You resort to contingency, which is only semblance,
but better than getting soaked to your unreal skin.

You post your stub to Metuchen and sleep through it.
The unreal wins. The rain stops. You walk clear

under reasserted stars through empty streets
that stink and are dangerous. Form. Instance. Sequence.

You wish you lived somewhere else. Is it worth cheating
to arrive nowhere? I ask, but where else is there?

Audit at Key West

You could put silver dollars on my eyes
and say I died of inflation. Strictly speaking
this isn't expense but unexpendibility.

Like being a crooked cop: I was last night
on late TV, but woke here unnegotiable.
How am I to sell out when no one's buying?

Somewhere a naked boy without bus fare,
and with nowhere to go, is bending over the bed
of a girl about to inherit her own body.

There are always investment opportunities.
But who breaks even? I might have been born rich
but couldn't afford the taxes. Perry was.

He died with a silver dogtag in his mouth.
In the cleft of his teeth. Everyone, Doc said, has one.
Eddie could spit like a B.B. gun through his.

But I don't want to start over. Suppose I could
spit bullets—what's a target? Last month in Frankford
we took flowers to the graveyard. A hundred names

spoke from their stones but we knew no one in town.
The house had been sold to strangers. The world is divided
into those who managed to buy in time, and their children

who can no longer afford to and must wait
for their parents to die. I'm willing in no hurry.
I have a book to finish. I'll put the contract

in the childrens' names. If there are royalties
—sometimes there are—at least I'll die a tax cheat
thumbing my clogged skull at the sons of bitches.

I carry a donor's card for what's left over
that could be any good to anyone.
If anything is. I doubt there is much left,

but the eyes aren't bad. Someone might still see
    something.
I'll leave a picture in them.—There, my Cuban
neighbor's fighting cock posed on the roof ridge,

a bomb of lit red fuses sputtering day.

January 1, 1973

If calendars are made of square holes, something
slipped a round-peg late March morning
into this opening. The dog and I
sniff wet-loam stirrings. I look for crocuses,
glad not to find: we're wrong enough already.

By way of omen, we're one second late.
Astronomers ticked it on to the last minute
of the dead year in their fussbudget accounting
of our eccentric orbit. As if one tick
could reason us to time. And yet in time—

in time enough—all seasons would drift loose
but for such finicals; as they did once
in Julian time, the Vernal Equinox
precessing through the centuries toward July.
We can learn to be more accurate than we have been.

Even corrected, we're wrong. If that tick's true,
morning rings false to feeling. A New Year's Day
smelling of wet roots? Let the dog run it
as if gifts were free. I thumb a forsythia bud:
is it too soft for this side of sun-shadow?

I mean to know. I get the pruning shears
and cut a stem to see if it will force.
Indoors again, I put it in a vase
and the vase on the mantel still decked out with holly,
the last dry scratch of Christmas. If this starts,

let the dog shed.—I may myself go bald
on gullied lawns—and leather apples shrivel
in the stubble of all season gone to random.
Just as it felt inside that astronomer's tick
between the year and the year, where Zero is.

Doodles

Except for abstract Liberty and Susan B.
(a failed design or a designed failure?)
we have never permitted women on our money.
Is this a matter of national character?

To be on money is to have nothing to spend.
We made a rule that you have to be dead to show there.
A wise provision. Think what we have been spared
of minority lobbying, incumbent assertion

—and humiliation: we were not born to labor
in whatever vineyard for a copper Herbert,
nor for an aluminum-alloy-sandwich Jerry.
Bread money must not be suffered comical.

We also decided, not by accident,
that the less a man is remembered for, the higher
his final denomination. Hamilton,
on the ten-dollar bill, is an exception,

a case of Treasury plugging for its own.
Even Treasury could work that scam just once:
Salmon P. Chase, another Big-T old boy
got shoved to the ten-thousand-dollar bill,

which is not in circulation. Soon now, perhaps,
there will be a trillion-dollar closed-circuit,
bank-transfer certificate. For it I nominate
Richard M. Nixon. Proportionately. And because

you have to be dead, which can be an advantage
when you might as well be. The surest way, of course,
is to be Queen of England. You then appear
on everything so often no one sees you.

—Except perhaps for the farthing (discontinued)
which went to the sparrow. No one noticed its fall.
No one notices faces on public issue
except when someone has been shoving the queer.

Then tellers check Jackson's eyes and Franklin's chins
as instructed by various agencies on guard
against the debasement of icons. Even then
the dead have nothing to do with how they are spent.

Kiss Me, Hardy

The last of the unabashed tragedians,
having out-ranted every other death scene,
choked on a fish bone at the cast picnic.

There are known fixed principles of malice
hooting gross as a peanut gallery
of Storm Troopers pelting deflected Shylock,

or a KKK convention out on the town
catcalling the rant of terminal Othello.
In the lowest Attic comedy well-hung

slaves were hanged naked, the ludicrous
erections of their constricted blood swatted
by clowns who flailed bladders and tossed quoits.

But that he who had resonated sententious
the deaths of a hundred kings and captains
should choke wordless while serious buffoons

pounded him on the back—it out-Barrymores
Barrymore, tip-tilts the snagged fly
that once did for the firmament, splits the seams

of der Rosenkavalier's great-butted pants
flashing a spot-lit drab of unwashed longjohns.
And through some black hole in the stage of space

keels over nose-first into the antipasto
to go to God with pimientos on his eyes,
anchovies up his nose, and for a tongue, salami.

Starlet

Tilda Trimpett and her seventh stage name,
having substarred and been left unconstellated,
OD'd on heroin purer than her habit
and died on her bed in a locked cube of mirrors.

When they found her twelve days later her toy poodles
had eaten a breast and part of a bicep to bone,
the exact details confused by liquefaction.
"Ah, Jesus, a sorry sight," said the cop the landlord

had called to turn the key for his lost rent.
The studio vouchered fifty-two dollars (exactly)
to get those damned let's-hear-no-more-about-it
poodles veterinized to their toy rest.

Secondhand Charley, in return for the mirrors
and the advertised bed, incinerated the mattress
and made a deal with Mendelsohn Morticians
for what they billed as "disposal cremation service."

Now and then on the Late-Late Milkman's Re-run
Tilda still smirks through portiers in Macao,
or sidewinds through tramp crews and sotted skippers
in the inscrutable haze of Singapore Sadie's.

Is there point in telling a ghost she couldn't have made it
in a thousand slinky crossings? She was not more tinny
than Harlow, say, or Grable, or Joan Crawford.
Tilda died knowing it's all in who you know

but made a wrong connection and went to the dogs.

January 2, 1978

My neighbor and his children are shoveling snow.
Or he is shoveling and they are rolling snowmen.
There is barely enough snow for shovel or play
and the sun will melt it, but for some, ambition
is an isometric and autotelic flexure.

Possibly, the sun will not melt the snow,
though my clogged gutters are already pelting
a rain on the back steps. If tonight turns cold,
my driveway may slick dangerous. Let it.
I shall be off to Key West in the morning

with nothing to care about anything until April.
If the house is here when I get back, I'll try it
for one more year. But it belongs to me,
not I to it, and I'm tired of working for it.
With any luck, a generalized inattention

should hold it together about as long as I
will hold together, after which someone else
can do as he likes with what I leave unshoveled.
I don't imply my neighbor is wholly an ass.
He is only young enough to want to do something

even when there is nothing. I sympathize
with most mistakes. One reason for Key West
is that doing nothing is an art form there.
And the fishing is good—precisely, I think, because
I don't much like fish, and don't care what I catch.

Exegesis of an Allegorical Text
XIII, 332. "What yearning fills me!"

So xiii, 1, "I yearn, therefore, I am,"
replies, reversing phrasing and numbering,
to i, 13, "I am, therefore, I yearn."

Meaning is what repeats itself once started.
Allegory is music, not rhetoric.
It does not speak; it listens itself to rest
through ambiguities of the echoing self.
So these last words, the echo echoing out.

On the narrative level, of course, Brave Archibald
has every reason to yearn specifically.
Dueling with Hated Bardo at Gate Twelve,
he is distracted by the usual vision
of Angelina weeping on the parapet.
His author-conditioned soul inevitably
"Soars like a fountain to her, flowing fixed."
And in that instant Hated Bardo strikes.

Now, in the dust, his amputated sword arm
still clutching Goodblade by him, Angelina
struggling to leap from the parapets but held back
by dwarfish servitors, while Hated Bardo
stands with Snicksnack's point against his throat,
Brave Archibald exclaims, "What yearning fills me!"

Be it noted that Hated Bardo yearns for nothing.
He has what has fallen to him, and most has fallen:
why else is he hated? In no particular passion—
as one might call for dinner, it being time—
he leans on Snicksnack, cutting off further remarks,
then masters Angelina, who comes surprised
to foreseeable conclusions. From time to time

he hacks a few more heroes as they come
and takes a few more Angels, each in turn
learning that beastliness is a sort of fun
girls can get used to. Later everyone dies,
no one more matter-of-factly than Hated Bardo
who yearned for nothing, and who never complained.

One Night on Lake Chautauqua
For Pat and Stasia

The lake, two miles out, was all fireflies.
You've seen those little glass domes that shake snow
where it's forever Christmas on the sleighs
forever arriving. As sure as arrival, I know
I was inside the one for the Milky Way.
Once in, some part of everything has to stay.

That's what forever is. One part, of course,
keeps squinting to see in. The drink in my hand
had been passed in from outside. From some lost source
I remembered there hadn't been one spark on land.
Yet here was this galaxy and we inside.
Galaxies happen as fast as they are wide.

Pat cut the houseboat engines and let in
the slopping silence. Adrift on my highball
I heard time tinkle and watched the glimmering
till a light flashed in my glass. So they do fall!
I scooped it and spread it on a kleenex to dry
till a waft flipped everything off to drown or fly

unaccounted in countlessness. That Milky Way
was wired to off-on switches. Whatever fell
blinked out between blinks, lost in that half-day.
Galaxies, from inside, have nothing to tell
but their googol-strew of lives as small as fizz,
each flickering whatever a life is

in its own glassed-in flurry, in a place
at the heart of habitat. As I, in the bow,
in a folding chair, one glassed-in hour of grace,
dazzled myself in the blink of forever-now
in the slopping silence inside inside. Till Pat
cut in the space-drive and swung back—from what?

The Limits of Friendship

For Joe, the sullen bastard

Dinner was duckling with tangerine sauce
and celery remoulade. He would not eat.
The wine was a classic Chablis from Wenty Bros.
He would not drink. Nor did he care to meet
the girls in the hospitality suite. "If you're flat . . ."
I offered, wallet in hand. He just sat.

Soon he began to stink. That made me nervous.
There are limits even to friendship. "That's dead enough,"
I said to the Armagnac and called Room Service
for a body bag and deodorant sprays. It's tough
to lose a friend, but pointless to hold on
after everything possible has been said and done.

At O'Hare

"You!" we chanted together. "How long has it been?"
"Twenty-five years," I counted. "A long time,"
he said, edging toward definition.
We stopped at a bar and edged closer.

But he was flying to Bozeman; I,
to Tallahassee. You can edge as close
as a second drink, a third. Sooner or later
it is time to start another twenty-five years.

Longer now. This time forever.

Nightmare

(The truth is dreamed toward morning.)

Just before dawn the world became a smother
of nothing but me. All up and down the street
my clone neighbors picketed one another
to preserve the neighborhood. I won't repeat
what accusations they bellowed face to face
in an apoplexy of accuracy. This race

can barely endure itself under pretense
of imagined differences. Now all was known.
Everyone guilty as charged with no defense
nor hope of mercy. Felon judging felon;
hypocrite, hypocrite; liar, liar. All
in perfect justice, each judge criminal.

I ran for the end of the nightmare and barbed wire
blocked me, dogs behind it fanged for blood.
I had been doomed to myself. "Liar!" I screamed, "Liar!"
And turned and struck. One fell and another stood
exactly as before, then two, then three,
four, five, to the end of numbers, exactly me.

"You know my reasons!" I cried. "They are yours, too!"
—Sooner shout to the bombers over Berlin
their last day's hammering. "All of you are through!"
I shouted. "The terror is over!" They bored in
like death abreast. The dream refused to break
no matter how I willed myself awake.

There was one last escape. I ducked inside
Hitler's bunker, nothing left in doubt.
If I could not stop their coming, suicide
offered the solace of wiping everything out.
I pushed the pre-set button and died through
to the holy city of barely bearable you.

Obsolescence

My wife, because she daydreams catalogues
and never knows what to give me (though, ah, she does!)
ordered for my birthday from Future-Now
an Omni-Function Digital Synchro-Mesh
Alarm-Chime wrist watch that beeps *Caro nome*,
(also available with *Vissi d' arte*)
though when I set it A.M., it beeps P.M.

I showed pleasure in her pleasure, and because
I have always accepted her choices, but when our son
seemed avid to borrow it, I let him keep it.
I know time only as a circle. Star time.
Rotation and orbit time. Dark and lit as tides.
He reckons it as a series of linear blinks.
He may be inventing a new code of perception.

Because I am obsolete, I cannot read it.
Or do not care to. Why should the old hound
stop sniffing and sprout wings? What is the scent
of the upper-air? I am rooted nose to ground,
circling and tracking memories of deep earth.
I nuzzle day and night on a dirt dial,
glad to die thoughtfully, in no hurry.

And to will him the many-tabbed side functions:
push for day, date, month, horoscope sign,
omen-computer, saint's day, point in orbit,
life expectancy, gross national product.
It could set its own alarm. By sonar scan
it could activate a robot whose eyes blink
the identity code of the successor species.

It could set itself to say: "At the sound of the chime
all circuits will be charged with induced Hebrew
in time to hear God announce the next illusion."
—I look out the window far as my father went
beyond the bird-limed sundial, and hear my son
—or something—ping in a solid state cathedral
programmed to project a 4-D God.

October: A Snow Too Soon

The mower just back from the shop. Chrysanthemums
more bud than bloom. Tomatoes red on the vine.
Yet down some shifting polar bulge there comes
this day-long ghost of snow. Enough to lime
the lawn as I haven't yet, as I half-thought
of doing but put off, and then forgot.

It melts at a touch on the hardtop, but the boughs
of the yews and hemlocks are brushed Japanese.
The car windows are soaped. A last red rose
is sugar-frosted not quite enough to freeze.
A not-much notably something. A bizarre.
Is it how much we are wrong, or just that we are?

Suppose a pelican lit on the roof peak
or the jungle-gym of the antenna: that
could only mean there's a ribbon in its beak
starched to some Omega-motto. But what?
It is never a pelican really, but a device
uttered in tongues, precisely imprecise

as omens gather. This could be the day
for trout in the eaves troughs. I will catch what I can
for no supper, and then sleep till May.
If the President phones, tell him there is no plan
sufficient to give sequence to unevent
—which has to be what the inscription meant.

On the Island

Wading a summer edge, a naked love
dabs a toe in the infinite, splashes back,
and we lie easy, one with the huff and shove,
ourselves a puddle of sea in a skin sack
dawdling in reprieve, the sea asprawl
in time to think. But nothing thinks it all.

We play beside a soft machine of seamless
self-joining rips and jostling hills. Off shore,
it is a grinder; deeper, by sun and moon stress,
a tidal heap; half-stone, a night-crush more
than bedrock but still parting to let down,
like a black mercury, into a million ton

last inch of itself, all that had once stood light
and prism-dazzled in the come-on flounce
of windy shoulders in the scarved bight.
But dress in all of it and every ounce
becomes a gravity. Or it slips loose,
redundant, palindromic, superfluous.

An acid, it eats everything but gold.
It boils off vapors and then sucks them back
in swirling slurps till, churning hot and cold,
it spins the hurricane down its howling track.
Inland a thousand miles it tolls a bell
out of its tower, reforming church and chancel

till rage is God and god an interval
in the maul of power that seems to have a cause
but not a reason. You can fill a pail
and wash the scuppers down in any pause
of demonstration, but all tidiness
drains back into original excess.

For nothing taken from it is itself,
nor itself less. From the last leadfoot deep
to its slipshod frothing on the coastal shelf,
it is the sum more than its parts, a sleep
of random particles engrossed beyond
all bells it breaks, all tenure, and all bond.

Credo

I asked the doctor who had pronounced me dead
to check his instruments. He owed me that much,
if only to escape my second opinion.
"What are you?" he said, "an enemy of the state?
My instruments have been federally certified."

I assured him I did not seek the overthrow
of force and violence. "I am a combat veteran,"
I said by heart. "I have received the vision
of the rose that blooms in bombsights. Yet I am pledged
to go on matching systole to diastole

more or less one to one. In sacrament.
By the power of which I beg to ask in doctrine
with the First, Fourth, and other revealed Amendments:
Can what you are trying to measure be measured by
what you are measuring with?"

                              —"Please spell your name
as you wish it to appear in the statistics,"
he said, gold pen in hand above a scroll
engraved CASE CLOSED. I spelled. "There is," he said,
"an optional blank marked *Comments*."—"I fantasize,
therefore, I am a fantasy," I avowed.

Even reading upside down, I recognized
he wrote an elegant hand. I will not argue
with elegance. Too rarely are we offered
that opulence more than wealth. "Amen," I said,
assured that every error must yield to style.

Useless Knowledge

To trap a chipmunk put a bait of nuts
in a glass milk bottle and lay it on its side
by a bush or a stone wall you have seen it favor.

The chipmunk will pop through the bottle neck,
fill its cheek pouches as if with Heaven's bounty,
and find there is no escape from the gifts of God.

By creature law, the chipmunk is forbidden
to spit from its mouth the nuts of life, once given,
until they have been brought to holy storage

in the ark of the winter covenant, and rather
than break commandment, this fluff of life will starve
with its pouches full and more food in the bottle.

A Vermonter from the bone-scraped ridges told me
that one starved winter's end he bottled a chipmunk
and filled the bottle with water to force it out,

but the thing drowned. He had to smash the bottle
to boil that ounce. He had no other bottle.
He said he starved through mud-time sick on roots

and curls of fiddler fern. He could have been lying.
Or stretching. But only God knows all His saints.
Something is always fevered by hard intention

for less than the wholely edible. These are notes
for a sermon on the sanctity of survival
to teach that life is not worth dying for.

But have we a choice? I have flown my hot missions
in a flammable bottle when I could have been grounded
on permanent garbage detail.* What's wrong with garbage?

those fragrant, bursting calories of revulsion
yardbirds can fatten on?—and damn the stripes
that jammed us lockjawed in the bottleneck!

All this may be as relevant as sainthood
inside a cyclotron. I haven't seen
a glass milk bottle since home delivery stopped.

If I could find one in an antique shop,
I could trap a chipmunk I would have no use for
and wouldn't know how to free without some danger

of killing or maiming it when I smashed the bottle.
This feels like something I know too well already.
It is useless knowledge, but what other is there?

*In the 73rd Bomb Wing aircrewmen who lost their nerve were no
good to their crews and were allowed to ground themselves, the enlisted
men losing their stripes and being put on permanent garbage detail. In
my ten months on Saipan, only two gunners in my squadron chose to
go on the garbage truck. I never knew anyone to mock them. There were
times, in fact, when I envied them the certainty of their stinking
survival.

Finally That Blue Receding Sphere

It is only after
you have hesitated too long
that the angel comes.

"No more time?" you say.
You are determined not to whimper,
but is this fair?

The angel shrugs.
"I am not exactly news," he says.
How drab he is!

"But why now?"
you insist. No whimper.
You are indignant with reason.

"Don't," he says,
"be tiresome." Yes, he is right.
You still wish

You had not hesitated.
"I love you! I love you! I love you!"
you cry back,

but the world
is receding faster than anything
can answer.

Where have you seen
this dwindling, blue-misty bubble before?
—TV, of course!

Among infinite rubbish.
What else makes him so drab?
At least you have said it.